Slim Goodbody's
GOOD HEALTH GUIDES

EATING RIGHT

By Slim Goodbody

Photos by Chris Pinchbeck
Illustrations by Ben McGinnis

Consultant: Marlene Melzer-Lange, M.D.
Pediatric Emergency Medicine
Medical College of Wisconsin
Milwaukee, Wisconsin

GARETH**STEVENS**
GS PUBLISHING
A Member of the WRC Media Family of Companies

Please visit our web site at: www.garethstevens.com
For a free color catalog describing Gareth Stevens Publishing's
list of high-quality books and multimedia programs, call
1-800-542-2595 (USA) or 1-800-387-3178 (Canada).
Gareth Stevens Publishing's fax: (414) 332-3567.

Library of Congress Cataloging-in-Publication Data

Burstein, John.
    Eating right / by Slim Goodbody.
       p. cm. — (Slim Goodbody's good health guides)
    Includes bibliographical references and index.
    ISBN-13: 978-0-8368-7740-3 (lib. bdg.)
    1. Nutrition—Juvenile literature.   I. Title.
  RA784.B78   2007
  613.2—dc22   2006032765

This edition first published in 2007 by
Gareth Stevens Publishing
A Member of the WRC Media Family of Companies
330 West Olive Street, Suite 100
Milwaukee, WI 53212 USA

Photos: Chris Pinchbeck, Pinchbeck Photography
Illustrations: Ben McGinnis, Adventure Advertising

Managing editor: Valerie J. Weber
Art direction and design: Tammy West

Printed in Canada

1 2 3 4 5 6 7 8 9 10 10 09 08 07 06

TABLE OF CONTENTS

Words that appear in the glossary are printed in **boldface**
type the first time they occur in the text.

Busy Body

Your body is busier than any **factory** on Earth. It is working day and night, week after week, year in and year out.

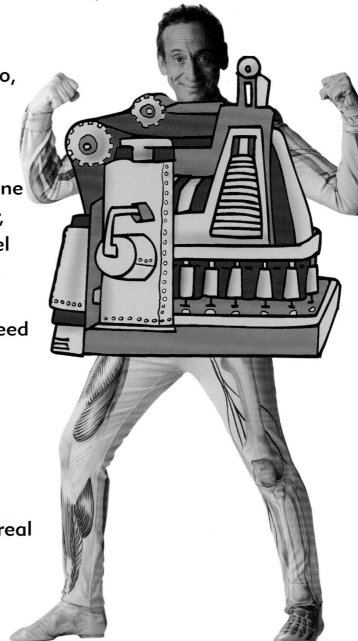

Every second of the day
And through the nighttime too,
Your busy body never stops
Working hard for you.

To do its job, to get things done
Through each and every hour,
Your busy body must have fuel
To give it strength and power.

What supplies this fuel you need
To keep your body going?
What provides this energy
To keep your body growing?

The answer is the vegetables
The chicken, nuts, and meat
The fruits and cheese and cereal
Yes, all the foods you eat.

Your body is always doing something. It might be doing something small like blinking or swallowing. It might be doing something big like running or riding a bike. If you tried, you could probably list a hundred things you do every day that take energy. Your list could include yawning, dressing, brushing your teeth, laughing, sneezing, washing, walking, playing, climbing, and skipping.

No matter what the activity, food supplies the energy to get it done. Everyone needs food to live and grow.

Let's learn about the many different things food does for you. You can also learn how to choose the right foods to help your body stay healthy and strong.

Something to Think About

Even at night while you are sleeping, your body keeps going. Your heart keeps beating, your blood keeps flowing, your **lungs** keep breathing, your muscles flip and flop you, and your brain keeps checking that everything is working well.

5

Built to Last

If you build a house, you need to use lots of materials. Wood alone will not do the job. You also need bricks, cement, nails, screws, steel beams, electrical wire, glass windows, and plastic pipes.

It also takes a lot of different material to build a body. The building materials for your body come from the foods you eat. Different foods do different jobs.

Some foods help you see better. Some foods help your skin heal when it is cut or bruised. Some foods help you grow taller. Some foods help you fight disease. Some foods are good for building stronger bones. Some foods give your muscles energy to move.

No single food contains everything your body needs. You need a wide variety of foods to stay healthy.

eyes

skin

bones

muscle

Something to Think About

You grow an average of 5 pounds (2 kilograms) and grow an average of 3 inches (8 centimeters) each year. Your body needs food to get bigger.

Break Down That Food!

Your busy body is made up of **cells**. Each of those cells uses some part of the food you eat. You have bone cells, muscle cells, **nerve** cells, skin cells, blood cells, and more. Most of these cells are really tiny. They are so small you could fit about ten thousand of them on the head of a pin! Before the food you eat can be used, it must be broken down into pieces that are smaller than cells. The process of breaking food down is called **digestion**.

Here is what your body does to digest food:

1 Digestion begins even before you start eating! It starts as soon as you smell food or see food that you like. You begin making spit (saliva) in your mouth that will help break down the food.

2 Then your teeth tear the food into smaller pieces. Spit gets these pieces wet so you can swallow them more easily.

3 These chewed-up bits move down a tube called the esophagus and enter your stomach. Inside of your stomach is **acid**. Stomach muscles mix the food with this acid and **dissolve** it into a thick kind of soup.

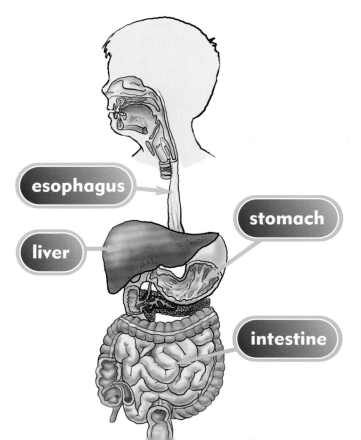

esophagus

liver

stomach

intestine

4 From here, the soupy food moves to your small **intestine**. This long, twisting tube is almost 20 feet (6 meters) long!

5 Other **organs**, such as your liver, send more acid. It breaks the food down even more.

6 Finally, the food has been broken into tiny pieces called **nutrients**.

7 These nutrients slip through the walls of the small intestine and get carried by your blood to all the cells of your body.

8 What your body cannot use, moves on to your large intestine and later on, when you go to the bathroom, it leaves your body.

Now that the food has been broken down, your cells have what they need to get their jobs done.

It is time for a cell-ebration!

100,000,000,000,000

Something to Think About
You are made of more than 100 trillion cells. That is such a big number that it would take you about 20 million years to count that high.

Team Nutrient

There are six kinds of nutrients. They form the team that supplies all the things your body needs. They are:

Proteins

Vitamins

Minerals

Carbohydrates

Water

Fats

Carbohydrates are your body's main source of energy. You get carbohydrates from foods like bread, potatoes, rice, spaghetti, fruits, and vegetables.

Proteins are used by your cells for building and repair work. You get proteins from foods such as meat, eggs, and beans.

Fats are packed with energy to keep you going. Fats also help build your brain and nerves. You get fats from foods such as vegetable oil, peanuts, butter, salmon, milk, and cheese.

Minerals help build strong bones and strong teeth. They also help your red blood cells carry **oxygen** and help your body fight disease. Almost all the foods we eat contain minerals.

Vitamins help keep your eyes and skin healthy, help cuts heal, and help protect against **infections**. Vitamins also help other nutrients work together. There are vitamins in almost all the foods we eat.

Water helps make up your blood, sweat, spit, **urine**, and **mucus**. There is some water in all the foods you eat, including watermelon, oranges, apples, and milk. There is even water in bread and meat!

To stay healthy, you need all six kinds of nutrients on your team.

Something to Think About

Sometimes people say we use food for energy like a car uses gasoline. However, that is only a small part of the story. Gasoline does not make cars bigger. Gasoline does not make cars stronger. Gasoline does not repair dents and accidents. Healthy food does!

The Food Pyramid

Most foods contain a number of nutrients. For example, pizza has carbohydrates, fats, proteins, vitamins, minerals, and water. No single food contains all the nutrients in the amounts you need, however.

This can make it a little confusing when you try to figure out what foods to eat. To help, the government created a guide called the food pyramid. It helps people understand how to choose a healthy diet. The colored stripes stand for the five food groups plus fats and oils. You need to eat foods from each different color group every day.

Orange **for grains**

Green **for vegetables**

Red **for fruits**

Yellow **for fats and oils**

Blue **for milk and dairy products**

Purple **for meat, beans, fish, and nuts**

Even though you need food from all the groups, you should not eat the same amount from each group. When you look at the food pyramid, you will see that some stripes are thicker and some stripes are thinner. For example, the orange stripe is thicker than the yellow one. The stripe's width lets you know you need to eat more grains than fats and oils.

You can also see that the stripes start out wider on the bottom and get narrower at the top. This shows that some foods in a group are healthier than others. For example, in the fruit group, an apple would be at the bottom of the stripe and apple pie would be on top. That is because an apple is a lot healthier than an apple pie. In the grain group, whole wheat bread would be on the bottom of the stripe and a cookie would be on top.

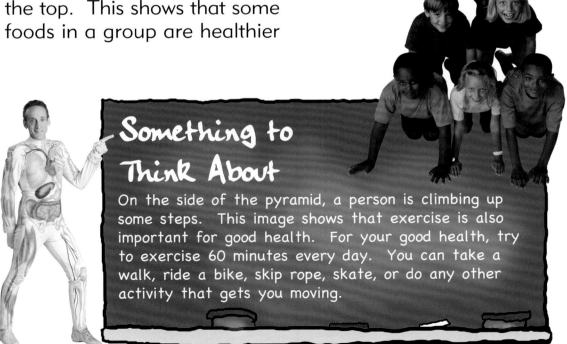

Something to Think About

On the side of the pyramid, a person is climbing up some steps. This image shows that exercise is also important for good health. For your good health, try to exercise 60 minutes every day. You can take a walk, ride a bike, skip rope, skate, or do any other activity that gets you moving.

Great Grains

The orange stripe on the food pyramid stands for grains. Grains come from plants like wheat, corn, rye, barley, rice, and oats. Most grains are ground into flour and then made into foods like cereals, bread, tortillas, and pasta.

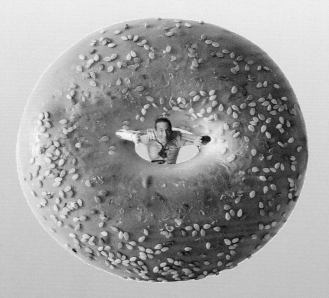

Grains can also be made into foods like cupcakes, donuts, and chips.

All grain foods are not equally healthy. To understand the differences, you need to know a little about how grain plants grow. When a grain plant is growing it has three layers:

The outer layer is called the *bran*. The main layer is called the *endosperm*. The smallest layer is called the *germ*.

Sometimes when grain is made into food, the bran and germ layers are left out. Only the endosperm layer is used for foods like white bread and white rice. These foods are found at the top of the orange stripe.

Sometimes when grain is made into food, all three layers are used. We call these foods *whole grain*. Some examples of these foods are whole wheat bread, brown rice, and popcorn. These foods are found at the bottom of the orange stripe.

Whole grain foods are healthier for you because they contain more nutrients. At least half of the grains you eat each day should be whole grains. A good way to eat whole grains is to eat whole wheat bread instead of white bread or brown rice instead of white rice.

To stay healthy, you must eat enough grains every day. Children who are eight years old and younger need four to five servings of grains every day. Girls who are nine to thirteen years old need five servings every day. Boys who are nine to thirteen years old need six servings of grains every day.

Here are some examples of what one serving equals:

1 slice whole wheat toast	5 whole wheat crackers
1/2 English muffin	1/2 cup (118 ml) cooked cereal
1/4 large bagel	such as oatmeal
1 pancake	1 slice white bread
1 small tortilla	1 cup (225 ml) whole grain cold
1 cup (225 milliliters) cooked pasta	breakfast cereal
1 hamburger bun	1/2 cup (118 ml) cooked brown rice
	3 cups (675 ml) low-fat popcorn

Something to Think About

People have been eating foods from grains for a long, long time. Scientists have evidence that people in **prehistoric** times ate grains for at least ten thousand years.

Vital Veggies

The green stripe on the food pyramid stands for the vegetable group. There are dozens and dozens of different great-tasting vegetables in this group. Here is a list of a few. The vegetables with a star next to them are orange or dark green vegetables. These are really, really good for you.

Artichokes	*Carrots	Garbanzo	Peas	Squash
Asparagus	Cauliflower	beans	Peppers	*Sweet
*Broccoli	Celery	Green beans	Potatoes	potatoes
Brussels	*Collard	*Kale	*Pumpkins	Tomatoes
sprouts	greens	Kidney beans	Radishes	Yams
*Butternut	Cucumbers	Lima beans	*Romaine	Zucchinis
squash	Eggplants	Onions	lettuce	
Cabbage	Endive	Okra	Spinach	

Vegetables can be eaten raw or cooked. They can be fresh, frozen, canned, or dried. You can eat them whole, cut into slices, mashed up, or in soup. They can be eaten in snacks and salads. You can even drink them in juice drinks!

It should be easy to get all the vegetables you need every day. Most people do not eat enough vegetables, however. That is hard to understand because they taste good and are good for you. Even if you do not like the taste of one vegetable, there are many others to try.

To stay healthy, children who are four to eight years old need one and one-half servings of vegetables each day. Girls who are nine to thirteen years old need two servings every day. Boys nine to thirteen years old need two and one-half servings of vegetables each day.

French fries are found at the top of the stripe. These should not be eaten very often.

Here are some examples of what one serving equals:

3 spears of broccoli

2 medium carrots or 12 baby carrots

1 large baked sweet potato

1 medium baked potato

2 large stalks of celery.

1 large ear of corn

1 cup (225 ml) tomato juice

1 cup (225 ml) chopped lettuce

Something to Think About

Vary your veggies. Even if you have a favorite, try eating another kind every once in a while. Each kind of vegetable has slightly different healthy nutrients.

17

Fabulous Fruits

The red stripe on the food pyramid stands for fruits. A fruit is a plant that usually grows on trees or vines. There are over one hundred different kinds of fruit! Here is a list of just a few. Some fruits you may have tried. Others fruits you may have never even heard of!

Abiu	Cherimoya	Grapefruit	Mombin	Plum
Akee	Clementine	Grumichama	Mango	Pummelo
Apple	Cherry	Guava	Nectarine	Quince
Apricot	Cranberry	Inga	Olive	Raspberry
Avocado	Coconut	Kiwi	Orange	Soursop
Banana	Date	Kumquat	Papaya	Star fruit
Biriba	Elderberry	Lemon	Pawpaw	Strawberry
Blackberry	Feijoa	Lime	Peach	Tamarind
Blueberry	Fig	Longan	Pear	Tangerine
Carambola	Grape	Mamey	Pineapple	Watermelon

Fruits come in many different colors, and it is important to eat a variety of different colored fruits every day. Almost anytime is a good time to eat fruit. At breakfast, you can eat bananas on cereal or blueberry pancakes. You can have a glass of apple juice with lunch. You can snack on an orange or some raisins after school. After dinner, try peaches for dessert.

Not all ways of preparing fruit are equally healthy for you. For example, fresh peaches have a lot of vitamins and minerals. They are found at the bottom of the red stripe. A slice of peach pie has less than one peach and a lot of added sugar and fat. It is found at the top of the stripe.

For good health, children need to eat at least one and one-half servings of fruit every day.

Here are some examples of what one serving equals:

1 small apple

1 large banana

2 large plums

32 grapes

2 small boxes of raisins

1 large orange

2 halves of a canned pear

about 8 large strawberries

1 cup (225 ml) of 100 percent orange juice

1 small wedge of watermelon

Something to Think About

It is very important to wash fruits before eating them. Be sure to rub them well with your hands under clean, running water to rinse away dirt and **germs.**

The Skinny Stripe

The yellow stripe on the food pyramid stands for oils. It is the thinnest stripe of all because you only need a little oil in your diet. It is very important that you get the oil you need, however.

Oils come from nuts, seeds, vegetables, fruits, and fish. You may already know some of them:

Almond oil	Corn oil	Kale	Safflower oil	Tuna fish
Anchovies	Cottonseed	Olive oil	Salmon	Walnuts
Avocados	oil	Peanut oil	Soybean oil	Wheat germ
Canola oil	Fish oil	Pecans	Spinach	
Cashews	Flaxseed oil	Pistachio nuts	Sunflower	
Coconut oil	Hazelnuts	Pumpkin seeds	seeds	

Oils help your body grow. They are good for your heart, your blood, and your brain. Oils provide vitamins and help you fight disease.

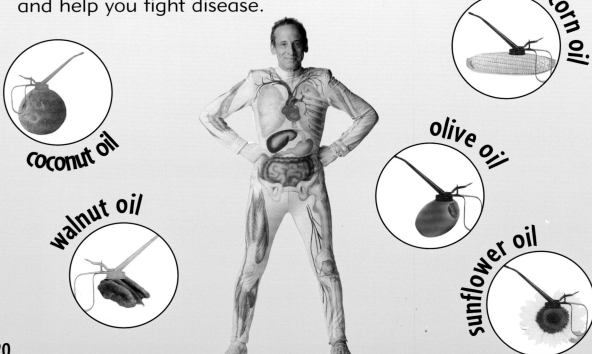

coconut oil

corn oil

olive oil

walnut oil

sunflower oil

To stay healthy, children ages four through eight need 4 teaspoons (20 ml) of oil every day. Children ages nine to thirteen need 5 teaspoons (25 ml) of oil a day.

You do not have to worry about getting enough oil because oil is in so many of the foods you eat each day. For example, peanut butter sandwiches, salad dressing, margarine, mayonnaise, or cashews all contain oil. Fish like tuna and salmon are also very good sources of oil.

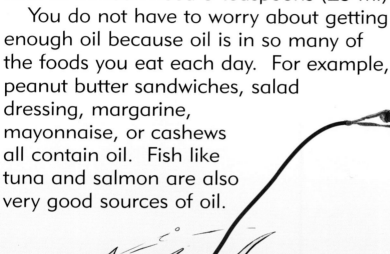

Something to Think About

The yellow stripe is a little different from the other stripes. Oils are not really a separate food group. They come from foods that belong in the other food groups.

Delicious Dairy

The blue stripe on the food pyramid stands for the milk group. This group includes milk and dairy products. A dairy product is a food made from milk, such as yogurt, pudding, ice cream, and cheese.

When you were born, milk was your very first food. As a baby, you probably drank a lot of milk. As a growing kid, milk is still important. Milk and dairy products supply your body with many nutrients that you need. For example, milk has calcium and vitamin D, which help build strong bones.

Dairy products can contain a lot of fat, however. Too much fat is not good for you. It is healthier to eat dairy products that are lower in fat. For example, skim milk, 2 percent milk, or low-fat cheeses are all found at the bottom of the purple stripe. Ice cream and butter are found at the top of the stripe.

Here are some examples of what one serving equals:

1 cup (225 ml) milk

1 regular container of yogurt

1 1/2 ounces (45 grams) cheddar cheese

1/4 cup (59 ml) cottage cheese

To stay healthy, you must eat enough dairy products every day. Children who are eight years old or younger need two servings per day. Children who are nine years old or older need three servings.

There are some people who cannot digest dairy products easily. They still need the nutrients, such as calcium, that milk provides, however. They must get these nutrients from other foods. For example, calcium is found in dark green vegetables such as broccoli and kale, fruits such as oranges and pears, and fish such as salmon and sardines. Lots of different nuts and seeds, such as hazelnuts and sesame seeds, also have calcium.

Something to Think About

Most milk and milk products we use come from cows. Many people around the world use milk that comes from other animals like goats, yaks, sheep, and buffalo.

Meat and More

The purple stripe in the food pyramid represents the meat and beans group. This group also includes poultry, eggs, peanut butter, fish, nuts, seeds, and peas. This food group is huge.

Here are just a few of the foods it contains:

MEATS	POULTRY	FISH	BEANS	NUTS
Beef	Chicken	Catfish	Black beans	Almonds
Ham	Duck	Clams	Chickpeas	Cashews
Lamb	Goose	Cod	Falafel	Hazelnuts
Pork	Turkey	Flounder	Kidney beans	Pecans
Rabbit		Haddock	Lentils	Pistachio
Veal		Lobster	Lima beans	seeds
		Sardines	Navy beans	Sesame seeds
		Scallops	Pinto beans	Sunflower
		Shrimp	Soybeans	seeds
		Snapper	Split peas	Peanuts
		Swordfish	Tofu	
		Trout	White beans	
		Tuna		

The meat and beans group provides lots of nutrients. One of the most important nutrients is protein, which helps build muscles, bones, skin, blood, and many other parts of your body. Another important nutrient is the mineral iron, which helps your blood carry oxygen.

At the bottom of the stripe, you will find lean meats, fish, and turkey. At the top of the stripe, you will find fatty meats, such as bacon.

To stay healthy, you must eat enough servings from this group every day. Children who are eight years old or younger need three to four servings every day. Children nine years old or older need five servings.

Here are some examples of what one serving equals:

1 egg
1 tablespoon (15 ml) peanut butter
1 cup (225) split pea soup
1/3 of a chicken breast half
1/3 small lean hamburger
1 slice of turkey
1 small handful of nuts or seeds

Something to Think About

Beans, peas, nuts, and seeds are part of this group AND part of the vegetable group. When planning your daily diet, you can include them in the group that works best for you.

Top Ten Tips

Here are some tips to help you stay healthy

3 Try not to eat foods with a lot of sugar, such as candy, cake, cookies, and donuts. Sugar has hardly any nutrients — no vitamins or minerals. Sugary foods can fill you up and leave little room for healthy foods. Too much sugar can harm your teeth and lead to **cavities**.

1 Start your day off right with a good breakfast. It will provide your body with the energy it needs to get through the day. One healthy breakfast could be a slice of whole grain toast, a scrambled egg, a glass of milk, and a piece of fruit.

2 Choose healthy snacks. Instead of potato chips, eat an apple or some sliced carrots. Instead of a candy bar, have a handful of raisins, a few whole wheat crackers, or a cup of yogurt.

4 Cut out soda. Most sodas have lots of sugar, and many have **caffeine**. Caffeine is a chemical that is not healthy. It makes your heart beat faster. It can make you jittery and nervous. It can give you an upset stomach. There are many healthier drinks such as water, low-fat milk, and 100 percent fruit juice.

5 Cut down on fried foods like french fries. They have a lot more fat than food that is broiled or baked.

6 Remember to eat foods from all the groups. That means every color every day.

7 Make sure that most of the foods you eat come from the bottom of the stripes.

BREAKFAST
LUNCH
DINNER

8 Eating all your meals is important. If you skip a meal or go without food for a long time, you can feel sleepy, hungry, or tired.

Then you might eat a sugary treat to fill you up fast instead of eating something with more nutrients.

9 At mealtime, chew your food well and do not rush to get finished.

10 Remember the staircase on the side of the pyramid. Nutrition and exercise go hand in hand.

Something to Think About

In the last thirty years, a growing number of kids and teenagers are having problems with weight. Today, 9 million kids ages six to nineteen are overweight. Being overweight means that they have more fat on their body than is healthy. A lot of that fat comes from choosing foods that are not healthy. For example, french fries make up about one-fourth of all vegetables eaten by elementary school children!

B-I-T-E

The better food choices you make, the healthier you will be. Here is a four-step plan to help you decide what to eat.

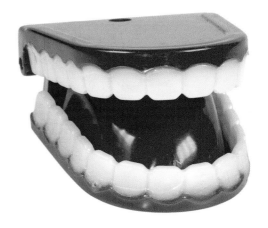

I call it B-I-T-E.

B — Before you choose, think about what would be healthy to eat.

I — Imagine how good you will feel about making a healthy choice.

T — Take action. Eat the good, healthy food, or sip the healthy drink.

E — Enjoy the taste and feel proud of yourself for making a good choice.

Something to Think About

Sample a new and healthy food at least once a week. It could be a new vegetable, fruit, nut, or seed. You might find it tastes great. Then you will have one more good food to help you stay healthy. Take one step at a time. You do not need to change your habits overnight.

The choices you make
About foods that you chew
Can lead to a stronger
And healthier you.
    I hope that by now,
It is perfectly plain
You need veggies and fruits
And good wholesome grains

Milk, cheese, and yogurt
Meat, nuts, and seeds
To deliver the nutrients
Your body needs.
    Foods that are healthy
Will make you a winner
At breakfast and lunch
At snacks and at dinner.

Glossary

acid — harsh chemicals that can break solid foods apart

caffeine — a chemical that causes the heart to beat faster

cavities — holes in teeth

cells — tiny units that are the basic building blocks of living things.

digestion — the process of breaking food down into nutrients needed by the body

dissolve — to break up and turn into a liquid

factory — a building or place where something is made with machines and people

germs — tiny living things that can often cause diseases

infections — sicknesses or diseases caused by germs

intestine — a long tube that carries food away from the stomach; it coils inside the abdomen

lungs — two organs in the chest that are used for breathing

mucus — a sticky, moist substance found in the nose and other parts of the body

nerve — special cells that join together and carry signals to and from the brain

nutrients — the chemicals that make up food, including carbohydrates, protein, fats, vitamins, minerals, and water

organs — parts of the body that do specific jobs, such as the heart, lungs, stomach, and liver

oxygen — an invisible gas in the air that animals need to live

prehistoric — describes ancient times long ago before people were able to write things down

urine — liquid waste the body produces

For More Information

BOOKS

Eating Properly. It's Your Health (series). Jonathan Rees (Smart Apple Media)

Food. DK Eyewitness Books (series). DK Publishing (DK Children)

Food Rules! The Stuff You Munch, Its Crunch, Its Punch, and Why You Sometimes Lose Your Lunch. Bill Haduch (Puffin)

Good Enough to Eat: A Kid's Guide to Food and Nutrition. Lizzy Rockwell (HarperCollins)

The Monster Health Book: A Guide to Eating Healthy, Being Active, & Feeling Great for Monsters & Kids! Edward Miller (Holiday House)

WEB SITES

Slim Goodbody
www.slimgoodbody.com
Discover loads of fun and free downloads for kids and parents.

Smart-Mouth.org
www.cspinet.org/smartmouth
This fun, interactive site helps you learn about nutrition. There are quick facts (called Snacktoids), recipes, articles, video clips, and games — all designed to promote healthy eating habits.

Team Nutrition
teamnutrition.usda.gov/Resources/mypyramidblastoff.html
Play this computer game and learn more about the food groups.

Note to educators and parents: The publisher has carefully reviewed these Web sites to ensure that they are suitable for children. Many Web sites change frequently, however, and Gareth Stevens, Inc., cannot guarantee that a site's future contents will continue to meet our high standards of quality and educational value. Be advised that children should be closely supervised whenever they access the Internet.

Index

About the Author

John Burstein (also known as Slim Goodbody) has been entertaining and educating children for over thirty years. His programs have been broadcast on CBS, PBS, Nickelodeon, USA, and Discovery. Over the years, he has developed programs with the American Association for Health Education, the American Academy of Pediatrics, the National YMCA, the President's Council on Physical Fitness and Sports, the International Reading Association, and the National Council of Teachers of Mathematics. He has won numerous awards including the Parent's Choice Award and the President's Council's Fitness Leader Award. Currently, Mr. Burstein tours the country with his multimedia live show "Bodyology." For more information, please visit slimgoodbody.com.